HOW TO...

Support your daughter through puberty

A practical guide for mums

By Melonie Syrett

With such love,
Melanie
x

First published by
Melonie Syrett in 2020
© Melonie Syrett

ISBN:
9798638676636

Contents:

Preface

Introduction

Chapter 1: For Mums

Chapter 2: Physical and Emotional Change

Chapter 3: Managing Menstruation

Chapter 4: Being prepared for periods

Chapter 5: Tips on supporting your daughter

Chapter 6: What to do when the first bleed comes

Chapter 7: Period myth and taboo breakers

Chapter 8: Relationships and intimacy

Chapter 9: Continuing support for your daughter

This book is dedicated to all of the girls attempting to navigate the world as they go through puberty and the mothers who do their best every day in supporting them. It is also dedicated to Susan Paul who helped me realise the expertise within me and bring it out to the world. Thank you Susan.

MELONIE SYRETT
Specialised Menstrual
Health Expertise

Preface:

This is a book for all mums and women who want to look after their girls as they begin the journey into puberty and periods.

It is intended to support the reader in understanding the facts and myths of puberty and periods and to build personal confidence so that conversations can be started, topics explored and fears quelled in both mum and daughter as you take this monumental step into 'little' womanhood together.

For too long the changes in the body and our periods have been hidden education.

They have mostly been whispered conversations between peers where untruths are given as fact. Some of us had nervous teachers who struggled with saying the words 'vagina' and 'period' and never uttered the word 'vulva' and unfortunately this continues in today's schooling.

The sensitive subject of growing up is rarely given the time it deserves and women for decades have reached adulthood not knowing the names of their internal reproductive system. Many have never felt comfortable looking at their vulva and have seen much of their body as 'not perfect' even though our bodies are all unique and therefore perfection is actually a myth.

All of this hidden nature feeds shame and taboo.

How many of us have slipped our tampon or pad up our sleeve as an adult as we attempt to visit the toilet without our bloody secret being uncovered? How many of us actually know what our cervix looks like and that our fallopian tubes are NOT actually attached to the ovaries? (I know, mind blowing!) How many of us grew up feeling that our friend's bodies were more desirable than ours? How many of us removed our hair because of perceived expectation to do so?
How many of us still do?

How many of us can actually say that we love our bodies?

This book aims to remove the myths and taboos of the female body and its processes and to enable mothers and key female caregivers to approach these subjects with their children with increased confidence.

In turn, the aim is to empower daughters to look upon their changing body with a sense of pride, preparedness, understanding and celebration of their unique bodies and ultimately their unique selves. It aims to help girls love their bodies and let go of shame.

I feel like this book should have been written decades ago.

I certainly needed it in the early 1990s. And now in the 21st Century, it can be a lonely place being a pre-teen and teen going through puberty.

With the free nature of pornographic material and Instagram filtered selfies, the pressurised lifestyle of being online all the time, plus the images we see of contoured faces, plump lips and bottom implants and the stats that even more young women are having labiaplasty – knowing who you really are and understanding that what you really look like is perfect, is an even more difficult and perhaps radical concept to grasp for our young people.

This book aims to change that.

Imagine what it would have been like to have the women you are closest to in your life walk alongside you, approachable and knowledgeable, as you took these first steps into womanhood. Imagine having someone to speak to, confide in and consider your options with. Imagine being able to raise the questions about changes in your body with people you trust rather than asking no one for fear of feeling 'different'.

Imagine if this person was your mum or sister or aunt.

I hope that this book enables mothers, aunts, nans, godparents, sisters and women in your life to support your girls and to make a difference for them.

And, when those girls are older and perhaps have children of their own, I hope that they will do the same, leading from the role models they had.

It is only by speaking about the unspoken that we remove stigma, shame and taboo and reclaim our sense of personal autonomy.

Loving our self and understanding our body enables us to really own ourselves – imagine feeling that you had the power over your body at all times and that you can choose what it does and doesn't put up with! With real body love we step into this sense of self.

Thank you for picking up this book. Just by reading it you are a change maker! By putting it into practice, you just might change the life of the girls you reach as well as your own.

They say it takes 7 generations to heal the pain and suffering of those in your line… Well, perhaps you are number 7. Perhaps you are the one who changes 'her-story' forever!

Introduction

My name is Melonie and I am an Educator and Specialised Menstrual Health Expert. I led Personal, Social, Health and Economic Education (PSHE) in primary schools for 15 years, showcasing my proven models of teaching tricky subjects nationally to MPs, Subject Association CEOs and Department for Education curriculum policy makers.

I shared my successes with parliament – speaking about the importance of high quality relationships education as well as training educators in the importance of normalising high quality teaching and learning around the sense of 'self' to ensure that young people are able to grow into successful and happy adults, whatever their vocational calling in life may be.

My specialism and passion is menstruation and menarche (first periods) which is taught poorly in schools and often lumped in with all of the aspects of puberty.

I left the school environment in 2017 to continue my work as an expert consultant for schools, organisations and local authorities and my menstrual based work with women and girls outside of education.

I was commissioned by City to Sea to create an educational programme focusing on Menstruation and in 2020 this work was fully funded by Waitrose and rolled out nationally for both primary and secondary school students.

I also work for the Real Period Project and we have been integral in creating the council's 'Period Friendly Bristol' Educational Guidance and the Hey Girls 'My Period' cards which are an amazing resource.

Why did I leave the education system?
I became frustrated with the way it was moving.

It had no time for nurturing young people as individuals and learning about your body was rarely of high quality.

Changes to the system pushed the already poorly taught PSHE completely off of the table – providing no guidance for teachers and schools. (The only guidance was printed in 2000 and has literally only just been updated).

It is safe to say that learning how we grow up – physically and in relation to others - has been bottom of the pile for the school system in the UK.

In the newest guidance, ready to roll out in Autumn 2020, the government has taken the 'Sex' part of Relationships and Sex Education (RSE) out of primary school altogether (which is where one might teach about puberty) and the only statutory school guidance on puberty is a small section in the Year 5 science curriculum!

Because of this low profile, there just isn't enough training for teachers in the area of puberty and so it is often approached by teachers, as it is by most adults, with a sense of fear and a lack of full factual information.

Parents too have shared their fears with me around how to approach this topic.

I received questions such as 'When should I speak about this?', 'Do you have a book I can use to help me?', 'How much information is too much?' 'How much is too little?', 'How can I talk about something so sensitive when I never had anyone share this with me?' and a lot of 'Will you do it for me?'

And I think this, for many, is where our problem lies. So many of us didn't have a person to speak to, someone to teach us the ways of 'woman'. We were left to it or given stuttered advice from a nervous parent.

Overall, there seems to be a fear around opening up and actively speaking about these crucial subjects in our society.

But if we don't open them up then year on year we unwittingly let down our children as they grow.

Year on year, more children go through bodily changes that they don't understand and as a result look to their peers or the internet for information. This often results in the increase of myth and taboo around the body and then ultimately more shame, more disconnect and less factual knowledge of the bodies we live in.

Alongside my work in schools,
I have been on a personal journey to reconnect with my own body.

My puberty and period education from home and school was negligible. My periods came at 14 and were always very heavy
and very painful.

In my late 20s I realised that as a teen I had developed some kind of body dysmorphia (I share more about this in the following chapters). I had really disconnected from my body as a young person and now recognised that because of this my self-worth was rock bottom.

As a result of this, I went on to attract partners (from aged 14 to aged 29) who either abused that vulnerability or mirrored it back to me in their own lack of self-worth.

Alongside this, at 27 years of age I was diagnosed with endometriosis. A horrendous disease that means parts of your womb lining grow outside of the womb and cause periods that have debilitating pain.

I spent my 30s immersed in alternative methods of healing. I learned to recognise and release self-hatred and to love and respect myself and my body again, which I hadn't done throughout my teens and my twenties, as well as healing my painful periods.
I was told there was no cure
for the endo but there was.

As a result of this life changing work, I founded a range of women's gatherings and events based around reconnecting women to their authentic selves in safe spaces.

I realised that many of the women I worked with were, like me, in some way disconnected from their bodies. Some had disconnected because they were unaware of the facts and stages of female life, unable to name their reproductive systems and ashamed to talk about their experiences of periods, peri-menopause and menopause.

Many of the women felt that they didn't own their bodies and as a result didn't put time into caring for their needs – be they physical (sleep, rest, time out) - or emotional.

One woman so truthfully put it recently, 'I feel like I'm coated in plastic', as she referred to her sense of being withdrawn from the world and her body.

I began opening up conversations on menstruation, peri-menopause, menopause, puberty, miscarriage, terminations, birth trauma and more.

As this work increased I became aware that so many women hold their pain and frustration inside and put their emotional needs aside.

So many women put up with not knowing what is happening to their bodies and why - as they age or push down trauma such as miscarriage - because it isn't spoken about in society.

The sense of what it is to be female and in a female body seems to have become taboo in the West with many girls having no one to speak to about their changing bodies as they go through puberty, begin their bleeds, start dating and then move into adulthood.

Those lucky enough to have had someone to speak to, often received part truths and accidental myth due to the lack of information around women's bodies available to those that taught them.

And so the cycle continues.

If we don't have the information as a child, and neither do those around us, we don't learn about our bodies and we keep our worries and problems about them hidden.

If we don't speak up about the body and our experiences then we repeat that as an adult. We don't seek to understand more as it is all hush-hush topics – unspoken, hidden and embarrassing.

And so, I seek to make a difference to the girls and women I work with. I want to nip this sense of disconnection in the bud.

I did as much as I could as a teacher and realise that now it is time to spread my wings and support others who have a huge impact on the way a young person grows up.

So, here I am. Starting with you the key women in girls' lives!

I strive to enable the world to understand the female body. To bring the processes that take place within the bodies of around half of the population into common, accepted knowledge - out in the open and part of everyday chat.

I believe that we can only do this by speaking about it and stopping it being hidden. And that starts with people freely talking about it to our young people – so they don't hold the patterns of shame and stigma that we did. So they make decisions based on their worth and health, not their desire to fit in. So they love themselves fully and hold themselves in high esteem.

I applaud you for picking up this book. For being interested in making a change. For wanting to support the younger generations in knowing their bodies and owning their sense of being female.

Chapter 1
For mums

Before we go into the facts and strategies for supporting your daughter, I think it is important that you take this chapter to think about you, mum. Please know that when I write 'mum' I refer to all the women who are 'mothering' or are 'big sistering' young girls. When I say 'daughter' I mean the young girls in your care or lives.

We women are always running around after everyone else.

We rarely give ourselves time to think and feel around a subject.

So right now I want you to do just that. Find a quiet place to read this chapter, one where you won't be interrupted. Perhaps grab a piece of paper and some pens or a journal and gift yourself this time to really feel into why you picked up this book by completing some of the activities below.

A good friend of mine, Julie Shekinah, used a term once that stuck with me. We were developing a girls circle to support girls in their journey of growing up. We unexpectedly ended up with a lovely group of 6 - and 7 - year - olds and part of our work was to run gatherings for the mothers and fathers so that they too could support their daughters around the work we were about to do.

Julie used the phrase:

'Treading the path before them'

and it switched a light on in my head and heart.

This is exactly what we wanted our families to do. To have already had the experiences that their daughters would be having in the future so that they too could support their girls from a place of having taken that path.

My thinking was this: When we have had experiences we come away with a sense of something. That something may be happiness and learning or perhaps embarrassment and distress. Often, due to no fault of those that were teaching us at the time – be they our close family, friendship group or educators - when it comes to puberty, bodies and blood we are often left with a sense of fear, rejection of what might be about to happen and shame. I would say that our history has been not to talk about the bloody processes of our insides and to keep them quiet and hidden.

**We know that we don't want this
for our daughters.**

We want them to love themselves and their bodies, we want them to be filled with wonder about what is coming next and who they will become, we want them to know that they are unique and that their bodies are perfect as they are. And we want them to know that if something doesn't seem right, no matter how intimate the body part, that they can and should seek support.

I invite you to take this time now to tread the path before your girl.

Perhaps go grab a cuppa before you begin...
And maybe some tissues!

Your first period:

I invite you to spend some time recalling your first period. Take yourself back there if you can. Close your eyes and bring the images and memories to your mind. Take time with each question. Don't rush through.

1.
Where were you?
Who was around you?
What were you doing?

Try and bring that image or memory
forwards.

2.

What was it like noticing your first blood?
Were you shocked? Excited? Fearful?
Who did you tell, if anyone?
How did they react?

3.

How did you manage the period?
What products, if any, were available to you?
Where did you get them from? Who taught
you about how to use them?

4.
What happened next?
Were you celebrated?
Welcomed into being a woman?
Did you keep it secret for a bit and finally share?
Were you able to speak about your bleeds with any of your immediate family?

5.
Were there any problems?
Pain?
Irregularity?

Perhaps take some time to journal this or create some artwork from what rises up inside. When you have finished just take a moment to notice how you feel.

Perhaps you have brought up some sadness or anger or a sense of happiness and joy.

We are all different and have experienced our menarche (first bleed) in varying ways. In my experience, most women I have spoken to have sad stories about their first bleed.

They felt alone, that their period should be hidden; some were paraded in front of the family and felt embarrassed and ashamed.

Others were taken to male doctors by their fathers and prodded about; some were away from their family and stuffed their knickers with tissue until they got home days later.

So many stories.

So many women.

Now bring your darling girl to mind...

How would you like her to experience
her menarche?

Perhaps in your journal or on some paper you
might wish to write what you want for your
daughter when she has her first bleed.

How would you like to speak to her?

What would you tell her about what is
happening to her?

How would you like her to feel if she notices
her first blood and is away from home?

We can't predict the exact date and time of her first blood but later in this book I'll give you some ideas on how to mark this massive point in your child's life in the way that she wants and in a way that increases understanding and excitement around this key time.

Remember I said about treading the path before them? By unpicking and remembering your first bleed and spending time recalling the feelings and actions and words around it, we bring to mind the good and the bad.

We know what we wished for and how we wanted things to be different.
And we begin to re-write the story for our girls as they step up towards this time.

Before you move on… If this left you with negative feelings and perhaps brought up sadness and shame it might be a good idea to hold a little letting go ceremony for yourself.

Perhaps grab a candle and a picture of you around the same age as your menarche. Take a pen and paper and write a letter to 'Little You'. Look at the picture as you are writing, tell her all the things she needed to hear at that time. Tell her how loved she is. How much you care for her. Tell her the information she needed and whatever else she needs to hear. Light the candle and read this to her – looking at the picture of you.

Allow yourself to sit with it for a little while and then decide what to do with the paper. Perhaps you want to keep it, perhaps burn it or perhaps bury it in a garden or special place.

Know that this honouring will make a huge difference to 'Little You'. You are effectively re-writing history by accessing the negative thoughts you laid down as a child and freeing them from your subconscious.

When you are ready you can move on to the next task.

The second task for you is about your own body image.

Puberty is a huge time. Our bodies change, our moods change, our hormones experiment with feelings of love and attraction and peer pressure is all around us.

Our body image takes a big shift at this time too.

Take a moment to really, truthfully say how you feel about your body to yourself right now.

Perhaps in front of a mirror as you look at yourself.

Maybe even without your clothes on.

1.
Do you like your body?
If so which bits do you like best?

Which bits are you not so fond of?
Why?

2.
Which parts do you think others like?
Why?

3.
Anything you might like to change?
Would you actually go through with those
changes?

4.

When you were young and your body started
to change, what was that like for you?

Here is a story about my body:

I was overweight as an 11 year old and taken to a nutritionist in my school uniform (funny that I remember that aspect so clearly). I saw someone from my school there too, in her uniform. I remember to this day who she was. I hadn't started my periods yet and I was unceremoniously confronted with this in the nutritionist's office.

'Have you started your periods yet?'
I felt like she demanded the information.

I didn't talk to anyone about things like that, we didn't as a family. I wanted to die. Let the earth open up and swallow me – anything to get away from this embarrassment, these people looking at my body and judging me, telling me I wasn't good and my body wasn't good, that I was fat, that I wasn't right.

On reflection, and knowing what I know now, I think I was probably just stockpiling weight ready for a growth spurt.

However, this well-meaning visit really damaged my sense of self. I know now that it wasn't anyone's fault, as my family thought they were doing their best for me. I was large. However, I was also very active and very fit.

I did grow and I lost weight.

At 14 I used to wear my best friend's clothes and she was gorgeous and slim, so I must have been of similar proportions. But I didn't see it. I saw a ball - shaped human. Like Violet Beauregarde in Willy Wonka and the Chocolate Factory when she expands... Except that I felt like that all the time.

I was also late to start my bleeds compared to my friends (aged 14) and I felt like the last one.

And it didn't stop there.
There were other things that really felt all consuming mentally.

Breasts... I didn't have breasts.

I would have done anything for a pair of boobs. My best friend had amazing boobs. My friends all had amazing boobs. Everyone had boobs except for me. It was on my mind all of the time.

From about 12 - 13 I wore padded bras bigger than my non-existent cup size. My mum told me once I wasn't the size cup I had asked for and that her boobs didn't grow until much later. I was with a friend at the time in the street. I didn't want to hear anything about how small my breasts were especially not in front of my friends from my mum! It felt like a dig. Like a direct go at embarrassing me in front of my friend.

It wasn't until I was in my late teens (17/18) that I grew the breasts I had longed for. But still my perception of them was that they weren't good enough. It was only in my mid-thirties with help from a rather enthusiastic partner that I realised my boobs were great. Desirable in fact!

I find it fascinating that I had held onto the perception that my body was too big and my breasts not good enough throughout most of my life. These opinions grew their roots at around age 11 and I still had them at 31+. And so, we return to you – grab your journal again

… What about your body?

1.

What was going through puberty like for you?
Did anything start growing or changing earlier
or later than others around you?
Was there anything you desired that wasn't
happening to you when it was happening to
others?

2.

Do you have any patterns or opinions around your body that you have had since puberty? Can you pinpoint the time that they began?

If you found a pattern or story or negative opinion I'd like you to try turning it around. Instead of 'I have a wobbly mum-tum' start saying something positive – I love the tummy that carried and grew my children'

Or
I have fat thighs – turn it to 'I love my thighs for all the places that they take me.'

Puberty is such a tricky time to navigate and we can lay down some really damaging stories that we tell ourselves about our bodies and our worth. It feels like it takes so much more time and energy to undo these stories and write new ones.

I wrote a story for myself that because I was overweight at one point, I was always overweight and because I had small boobs I was less desirable than my friends.

This story was laid down in a matter of months, a mere few occasions where things stuck out, like the trip to the nutritionists.

It is crucial that we walk the path with our girls; supporting them in laying positive foundations and positive stories around their body image, self-esteem and living as your authentic self.

If we write the original story well, then there is no need to re-write that bit later on, is there?

Treading the path before our girls can really help us see that the timing of what they learn and the models that they have around them, including the words that we use, have huge impact.

Now – let's get on to ensuring that our girls have the facts that they need.

Chapter 2
Physical and Emotional Change

This chapter will go through the physical, mental and emotional changes that happen during puberty. This is for your benefit so that you have all the information and can confidently speak to your girl about her body and how it will change. Use it as a reference book, come back to it when you aren't sure of an answer and re-read sections when you feel like you will be chatting with your daughter.

Each section is split into two parts – facts and common concerns. These concerns are things that children often bring up when I'm working with them and I offer some options for supporting your child.

There are additional techniques for how to speak to your children in chapter 5 - particularly about what to do when you don't know how to answer a question! Menstruation is expanded upon in the next chapter.

Puberty - Facts

The term puberty refers to the process of physical changes that take a child's body into sexual maturity. Sometimes the term is linked with the perception of 'becoming an adult'. Puberty is a long process. It starts at around 8 years old for females and a little later for males. Puberty can continue to around 17 years of age.

The young person's brain and gonads (testicles or ovaries) act like switches turning on sending messages to the body to start different processes.

The most important fact of puberty, in my opinion, is that it doesn't happen to young people all at the same age. Every single body is unique and has its own clock. The switches turn on according to their clock, not anyone else's. This is why we get that real variation in young people around the ages of 8 -13 years and onwards.

Common Concerns

My work with women and girls has opened up this conversation around 'adulthood' and the pressure that young people can feel to leave their childhood behind.

I feel that many young people have carried a sense of 'not wanting to let go of childhood' with them into their adulthood. I believe that a child going through puberty who starts their periods cannot be expected to carry such a burden. They are not adults. In the eyes of the law they are not adults until they are 18. They can't get married and have sex legally until they are 16.

It's time to rephrase what puberty is. Yes… it's the process that the body goes through to enable it to make and grow children. That is a biological fact. But perhaps the words we can use with our children are:

'Puberty is the process of the body getting ready to become an adult.'

Rather than saying once you have gone through puberty (or its key markers which are seen as starting periods for girls and for biological males, wet dreams) you are an adult.

It isn't much of a semantic change but it is enough to feel that weight of leaving childhood behind and the expectation of having to be a 'grown up', lifted.

As this book focuses on the biologically female body, I won't be going into male bodies here (But there will be a book out soon to help mothers in supporting their boys through puberty. There will also be a book that you can give to your girl that will complement the information that you find here.)

Let's have a good look at what happens during puberty for our girls.

Underarm and Pubic hair - Facts

Often one of the first signs that puberty is beginning is the arrival of a few wispy hairs in the pubic region and breast budding. The hair starts off quite downy, can fall out and go back to being bare for a bit before coming back, but get thicker and darker as the body matures. Underarm hair tends to come a little later.

Pubic hair and underarm hair can grow straight or curly, dense or sparse. The colour is often similar to the head hair but not always the same.

Common concerns

In my experience, the top issue around puberty for the girls I have worked with has been hair.

Often the first thing that comes out of their mouths is about how they can remove it. This comes from girls around the age of 10 and 11.

I reflect, often as I am speaking to girls, about how much of our female hair growth goes unsaid. Even to our best friends and partners. So many of us have hair in places that we just don't talk about.

How many of us adult women have hair on our chins and top lips, on our cheeks, our chests and around our nipples, under our belly buttons and lower bellies, on our thighs and little places like on our toes that we don't like to mention?

Perhaps our beauty therapist or threading specialist or laser removal person is the only one who sees our truest selves!

And here is where I introduce my mantra –

'If it is hidden it becomes taboo and stigmatised'.

If we don't see it and we don't talk about it then it becomes something undesirable, something wrong.

Porn, underwear catalogues, music videos, social media, billboards and the like usually show NO hair. Not a strand wisping out of the side of a bikini, or a shadow on a top lip. Nothing. And our TVs are awash with adverts for hair removing products.

The world says to us daily – remove it. This is what our lovely children see and believe is true unless someone shows and tells them otherwise.

I am lucky enough now (at the age of 39!) to inhabit a friendship circle where many women are experimenting with growing their underarm, pubic and leg hair. When I was at school this was just not a thing.

I remember shaving for the first time in secret and slicing half my leg like I was planing wood! I was given my first box of Jolene to bleach my darkening 'tache at about 12/13 and burned my face where I wasn't mixing it correctly. I was also urged to have electrolysis because it had longer lasting effects.

Over my life I have had battles and befriending sessions with my hair. I'm from hairy stock. I have a moustache, chin hair, and a lot of leg and armpit hair, a snail trail (which I remove) and my belly hair and arm hair are darker than I would like. I also have wild pubic hair that makes a trail down my thighs (which I don't tame anymore) plus other hair I don't fancy sharing with the world.

Over the years – oh my word – I tried so many ways of removing it! Waxing, electrolysis (nobody told me at the time that the body goes through cycles and it would all come back), threading (ouch!), shaving, bleaching, epilating (yuck!) and more. I even had laser therapy on my back as there was a patch of hair that I thought was too dark and I wouldn't wear a low back top- ever. That made me scar as I have sensitive skin.

As a teen I thought every woman had lovely tight curly pubic hair that is a gorgeous triangle shape and frames the vulva beautifully.

So can you imagine my fright when mine came out all long and straight and it couldn't be sculpted for toffee. Cue shame and home waxing episodes. I just thought 'My pubes don't look right!'

I think now people have hairy armpits more often and sometimes I have experimented with growing my hair.

I think the mind – set that we need to adopt and promote regarding hair growth is 'It's my hair, it's my choice.' And that these choices need to be made for ME, not to please society or a partner.

For your girls, when talking about hair growth it is important to share that all of our hair is different. Tell them how it grows at different rates, at different times, in different shades and lengths and thicknesses and in any form of straight to tightest curls. Pubic hair and armpit hair are the same.

They will grow in the way that they grow for you – the owner of the pubes and pit hairs.

You may also wish to share that throughout their life their hair might change too and other hair might pop up in other places. Hair grows in all kinds of places on all kinds of people. The only places you won't see it are the palms of your hands and the soles of your feet. Even your nose has hair ON it! Look closely...

Breast Formation - Facts

The breasts grow in a few stages. The first stage is breast 'budding'. With this the nipples become puffy and it can feel like there is a 'bud' underneath the nipple. It can happen to one nipple first and this is normal. It can be a little painful.

After the budding the next stage will begin which is the formation of the breast tissue. This can take many years and there can be many growth spurts until the breasts finish growing.

They begin with the tissue below the breast beginning to develop. Then around the breast before the main breast shape takes formation. These growth spurts may include growing pains. The growing breasts may be sore or raw feeling. Wearing soft clothing can help with this tenderness.

The nipple colour will also darken throughout these growth stages.

Some girls have inverted nipples for a time. These usually right themselves without intervention.

There may be the formation of little bumps around the areola (the skin around the nipple). Sometimes these are hair follicles around the nipple or oil glands. These are normal but rarely spoken about.

Breasts grow in all shapes and sizes. One is often a little bigger than the other – again this is normal. There is no 'right' size of breast.

They can also have lumpy breast tissue underneath. It is useful for girls to get to learn how their breasts feel throughout their menstrual cycle. They may find that they are lumpier just before and during menstruation and that the lumps reduce after menstruation. Like any body part, if there are lumps that don't go away and are worrying it is worth going to the GP to get them checked out.

Common Concerns

'Mine don't look like everyone else's'

There is a real worry as the breasts begin to grow around 'what is a normal shape and size?' The answer is that all breasts are unique and all nipple shapes are unique.

Some are big with large nipples, some big with small nipples. Some are small with big nipples; some are small with small nipples. Some nipples stick out a lot; some don't stick out at all. Some look puffy, some look flat. Some clearly change with the weather or arousal or excitement... Some don't!

Some girls begin their breast growth very young and they can worry that they won't stop growing.

If your daughter has large breasts it is possible that she will feel self - conscious about them. They can attract unwanted attention.

Supporting her in knowing that they will stop growing and providing appropriately supportive underwear and clothing will help. Ensure that you are aware of her body sensitivity and support her in feeling comfortable.

Sometimes you can predict breast growth by looking at other family members and whether there is a trait in size but it is important for your daughter to know once again that her body is her body. It will grow and change when it wants to and in the way it wants to. It may buck the trend!

As mentioned before, one of the biggest things on my mind as a teen was that I had no boobs. I used to pray for them! I wanted them! I felt so aware that I didn't have them that it stopped me doing a lot of things. If someone had said to me, 'your body is your body, it is doing what it needs to at the time it thinks is right' it may have helped me feel less different to my peers. I also felt less desirable to boys.

My friend had huge breasts and I felt that my lack here stopped me getting boyfriends. It would have been good to hear at 15 or 16 that my body is normal and that attraction comes in many forms. People are attracted to people for many different reasons.

Height and Weight - Facts

As a girl's body prepares for the onset of menstruation she will find that it stockpiles some fat which can mean that her shape and clothing size change. This is because fat reserves are necessary to help start the menstrual cycle.

Usually, after the onset of menstruation, the fat reserves are no longer needed and your daughter's weight will even out again. This can sometimes happen before a height growth-spurt, too.

Usually girls go through a few height growth-spurts as they go through puberty. The body can therefore go through a few changes before settling in to what might be the body shape she grows into adulthood with.

Common Concerns

Body weight can be a tricky subject for a young girl who is facing all of the other changes that come with puberty. It is also a noticeable change and can attract unwanted comments.

Ensuring that girls know that their bodies are likely to change throughout puberty can help them understand that their body is likely to change further once they begin their periods. It will also help them see that their periods are likely due soon.

It's good to avoid talking about any personal insecurities around your daughter.
I had a friend once who always complained about her legs. She would look in the mirror, holding her legs, looking at them, saying how big they were, saying she couldn't wear this or that as they were too fat.
At about 7 years old her daughter started saying the same. It caused so much upset – to mum to see her daughter upset - and to the daughter because she felt her body was wrong.

As hard as it is to be mindful of what is being said, I urge you to curb negative self-talk or distasteful looks in the mirror around your daughter.

It can have the effect of encouraging her to pick out parts of her body to dislike or wish to change. This also goes for dieting and the like.

When we are only showing what we don't like and want to change, we are reinforcing that our body is not good enough - that there is a perfect model to be.

Which we know is not true.
Speaking in a body positive manner around her about yourself and other women could help reinforce positive feelings about herself and her uniqueness. We all know what it is like to suffer a blow to our self-confidence and body image.

You have read the example earlier of my sense of size blowing up out of proportion (pun intended) after the visit to the nutritionist. The effect it had was life-long.

As a teacher I heard many children talking about having fat stomachs, thick thighs and the like and wanting to change them.

I also heard girls picking on what other girls looked like. 'She is fat', or, 'She is too hairy'.

When I say this I mean children of all ages - not just puberty age. Sometimes children in the role play corner aged 4 would be saying it as they played 'mummy' in the mirror or talking about their bodies and ending it with '… like my mum' to their peers.

I know it is hard, as we see the things we feel are flawed more than anyone, but if you can avoid your own negative body speak around your daughter then you will do her the world of good. If you have a positive home environment around body image then your daughter will have a solid foundation to come back to, even when things are said or perceived as negative away from home.

You can also open up the channels to speak about the body together. Provide that safe space to explore what she likes and doesn't like about herself at the moment. Then you can talk about the possibility of continual changes, as she goes through puberty.

Waist and Hip Shape Changes - Facts

Both male and female bodies change in shape as they go through puberty.

The most obvious after breast growth is the development of a more 'adult' shaped body as compared to the quite straight up and down body of a child.

As with anything to do with puberty, the change in body shape is unique to the girl.

Looking at the body shape of mums, aunties, sisters and grandmothers can provide a possible idea but are not definitive measures.

What tends to happen to most girls is the formation of a waist and the widening of the hips.

Common Concerns

Whenever I work with girls and boys their drawings of girls that have been through puberty end up with hourglass figures!

It is like somehow this shape has become synonymous with being a grown up woman. We know that body shapes come in so many different variations and that hourglass is just one of these.
It is useful, when talking about body shapes and having images of women in photos and artwork, to try and share the range of shapes a female can end up with and emphasising that each of these are perfect.

Smashing the myth that one is more desirable than the other's will help your girls feel confident in their skin.

At around 14 years old, I noticed that I have quite a square shape. My back is square.

I felt aware of this at a swimming gala (I mean I was also aware that my luminous pink cossie was see through and I had no boobs and I was the only girl in the breast stroke race, but you know, I smashed it!) It was on my mind for some time.

That my shape wasn't what the mannequins had and my clothes hung differently to others.

As an adult, I know that we are all different and my shape is my shape. But I think if I had someone to speak to about it and positive images around me, this wouldn't have been a 'thing' that caused me to waste energy thinking about it.

Spots - Facts

As oil production and hormonal surges increase so can the production of spots. However, the intensity of spots is highly individual. Some girls will get one or two here and there, others will have outcrops of acne that persist.

The skin has sebaceous glands which produce sebum. These glands can over produce during the teenage years and become clogged.

Some girls will get spots on their chest, neck or their back and shoulders.

Blackheads can form – these are usually clogged with dirt and other material and whiteheads can form – these are usually pores clogged with oil and skin and covered by layers of skin.

Androgens –which are a hormone that increases during puberty and plays a role in the menstrual cycle - can also widen pores and increase sebum production.

Common Concerns

Spots can be painful and can make people feel self-conscious. Many girls choose to pop them and use a range of products and old wives tale ointments to try and get rid of them.

Knowing that spots, like any other puberty occurrence, can manifest in a range of ways on different people can support girls in feeling comfortable if they find themselves with more spots than their peers, although they can still affect their perception of their appearance.

Ensuring that your girl washes daily will help her to remove dirt from the skin.

Something often prescribed at the GP is the contraceptive pill as it works on androgen production.

I would suggest reading 'The Pill – are you sure it's for you?' by Jane Bennett and Alexandra Pope before making the decisions on whether your girls should take contraceptives, especially for the skin.

Discharge – Facts

As a girl gets closer to her first period she is likely to notice discharge in her knickers and when she wipes herself after going to the toilet. Discharge is the name for cervical mucus.

This little talked about aspect of femininity is characterised by a cycle of differing discharge textures and colours. This links to phases of the menstrual cycle.

After menstruation the discharge can look creamy and thick, towards ovulation it becomes more slippery, watery and see through, after ovulation the discharge becomes thicker and can become crumbly before disappearing altogether before menstruation.

This pattern returns with every trip around the menstrual cycle and adult women can use it to track their most fertile times.
It is normal to have discharge.

Common Concerns

Many girls don't even want to talk about their discharge as it seems embarrassing to them, especially if no one has ever spoken about such things before. Creamy knickers aren't really what you want to own up to as a kid if you're from a place where this kind of stuff is not spoken about.

It is important for them to know their body will make discharge and that it is normal and happens to every female.

I like to share this information when I'm speaking about periods and the menstrual cycle as it is a key factor of the cycle. It makes sense to talk about it then rather than in isolation.

It is also worth sharing with your girl that this discharge can create that little white 'bleaching' in the knickers. Again this is normal.

Girls should know that if the colour of mucus takes a green tinge or smells very bad then they should seek help. There may be an infection present or a disruption in the ph. levels of the vagina.

Many women and girls suffer from thrush or bacterial vaginosis. Thrush is characterised by cottage cheese – like discharge and an itching, burning sensation. Bacterial Vaginosis (or BV as it is often known) is detected often due to the strong and unpleasant odour it emits.

Sometimes the cause of these can be tight, non – breathable clothing. It is worth checking that underwear is made of cotton and that the clothes are not too tight.

Periods - Facts

Periods are the result of a full menstrual cycle. They are the releasing of the lining of the womb at the start of a new cycle.

Where is the womb?

The location of the womb (also known as the uterus) is around 3-4 fingers width down from the navel. It is around the size and shape of an upside down pear. The bladder sits in front of the womb and the rectum is behind the womb.

Below: Diagram showing approximate location of the womb within the female body

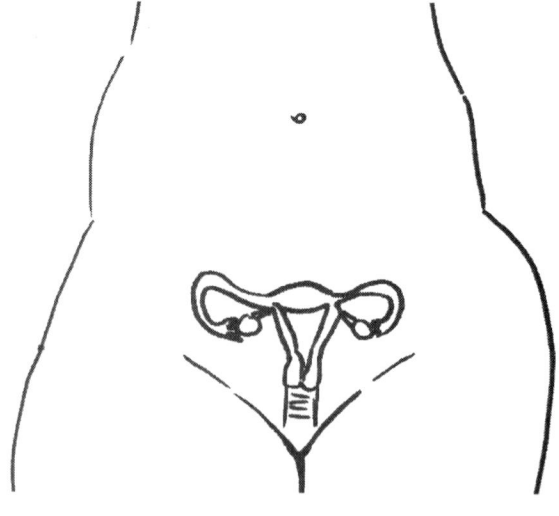

Below: Diagram of the female internal reproductive system.

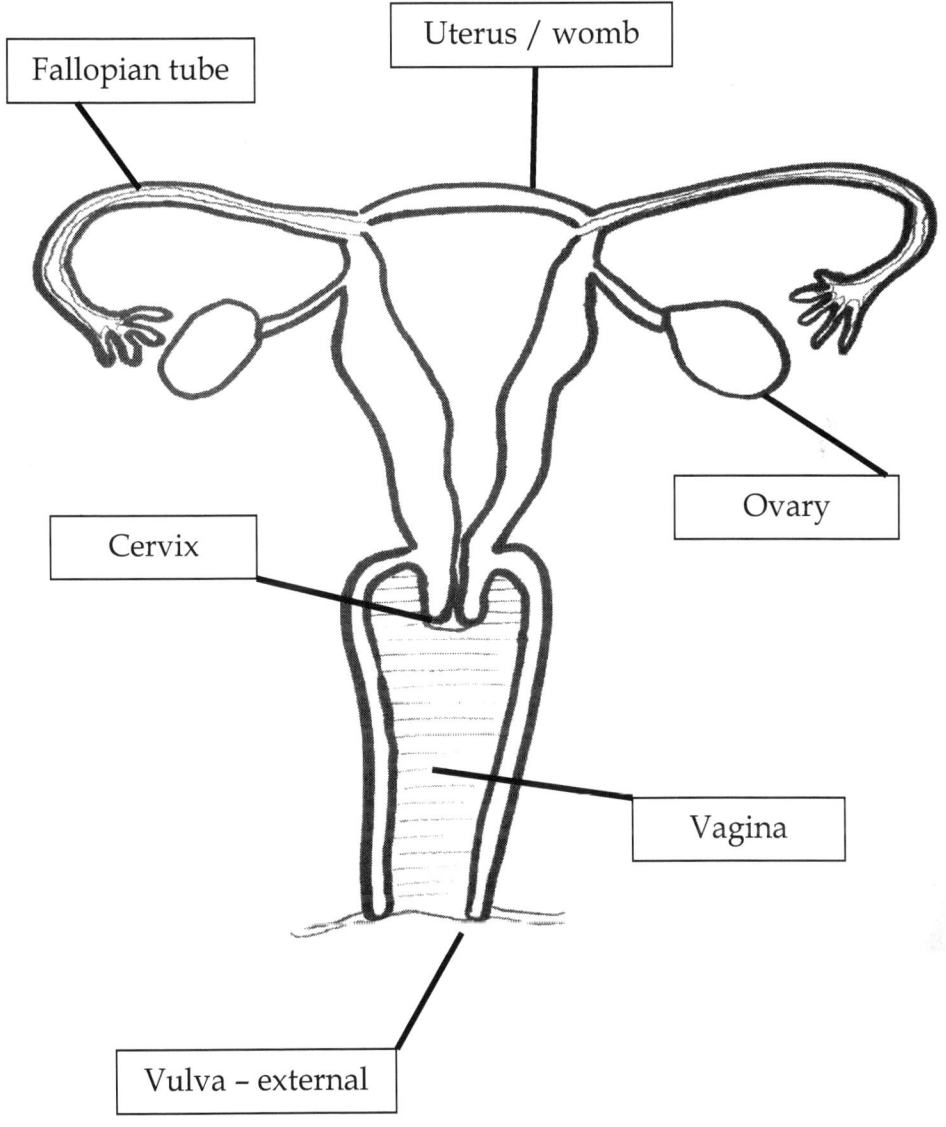

Uterus / womb

Fallopian tube

Ovary

Cervix

Vagina

Vulva – external

The womb has fallopian tubes coming from either side of its top edge.

The ovaries are not attached to the fallopian tubes. They are attached to the womb by a ligament as can be seen from the diagram. These contain the millions of immature 'ovum' or eggs that a girl is born with.

The top of the womb is called the 'fundus'. The cervix is the bottom of the womb and is often referred to as the 'neck' of the womb.

The cervix is the opening of the womb and menstrual blood passes through the hole in the cervix, down the vaginal canal and out of the body.

It is the cervix that is swabbed during a cervical smear. The cervix has little channels within it that create cervical mucus or discharge.

The external genitalia are collectively known
as the vulva.

The vulva is made up of the Mons pubis, the
labia majora and labia minora, the clitoris and
the vestibule (which is the opening to the
vagina and the urethra.)

Below: Diagram of the female external
genitalia – the Vulva

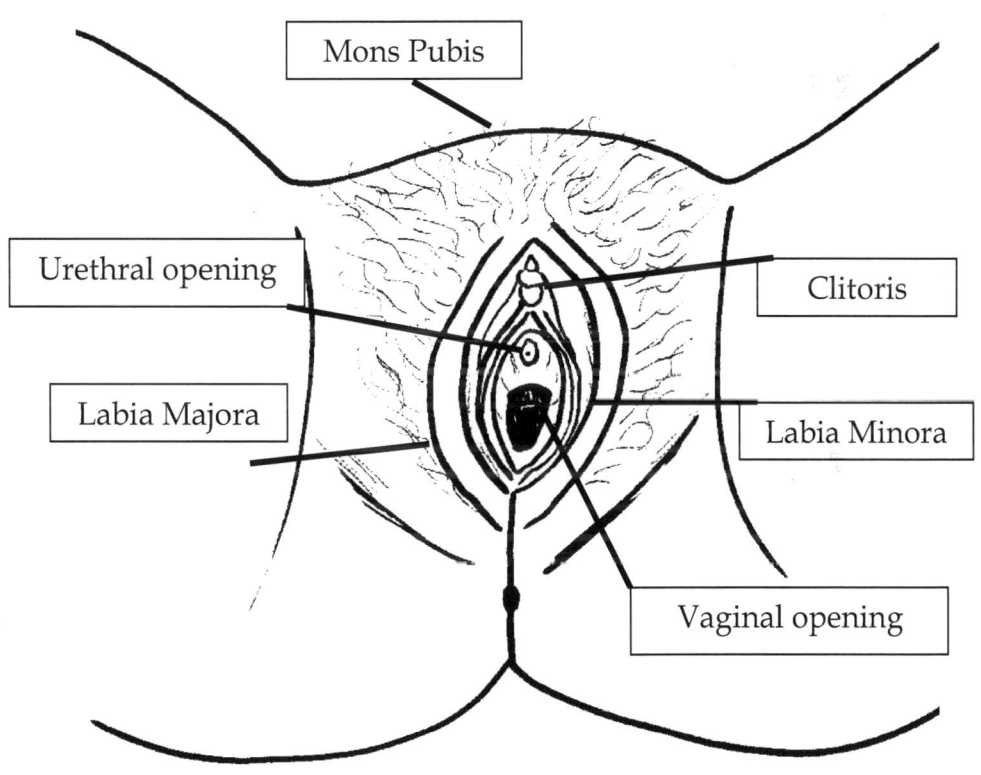

The menstrual cycle can be split into 4 phases

Menstrual phase – the lining of the womb is released. This usually takes around 3-7 days. The flow of blood is usually heaviest on days 1 and 2 and it begins to reduce in flow towards the final days.

Pre-ovulation phase – After the period the body starts to prepare to release an egg. The ovaries send some of the immature eggs to their outer walls where the eggs begin to ripen in follicles, or little cysts. One egg usually matures more than the others. At the same time the lining of the womb begins to build up its tissue again.

Ovulation Phase – The mature egg is released from the follicle. The other eggs are reabsorbed into the body. The end of the arm of the fallopian tube, called the fimbriae, collects the egg and begins to pass it down the fallopian tube in preparation for fertilisation. The lining of the womb continues to thicken for a fertilised egg to implant into it.

Pre-menstruation phase – If the egg is not fertilised it begins to break down. The lining of the womb is no longer needed and it too begins to break down. This leads back to the menstrual phase.

Periods can begin anytime from around 9 to 16 years. The average age is around 12 - 13 years. The first bleed is called 'menarche'.

Often the first bleed is brown and many girls believe that they may have soiled themselves. Brown blood at this time is normal.

It can take quite a few months for periods to reach a regular pattern after menarche.

It is useful to record the first day of each bleed on a calendar or in a diary or a period App. This will help your daughter notice patterns in her cycle. It is normal for a menstrual cycle to come every 25-33 days. It is also normal for it not to be the same amount of days each month.

Charting cycles helps see the average for your daughter or her regular patterns.

I track my cycle and know that anything between 28-33 days is normal for me. Last January and February were not in the norm. I am 39 and did wonder if this was the beginning of a peri-menopause journey.

There is a list of apps and charting sheets in the resource section at the back of the book.

Common Concerns

'Will people know I have my period?'

Lots of girls worry about others knowing they are on their bleed - particularly as they are so aware of it at the beginning of their menstrual life.

It is important to let them know that people can't see their products, they won't know by the way that they are walking that they have a pad in their knickers and the only way that anyone else will know is usually if you tell them.

'What if I leak?'

This is a huge concern for girls. I find it most beneficial to say that everyone who has a period will leak sometimes.

As you get used to how your blood flows you can use products to support the collection of blood more efficiently. Even so, there will be times you leak into your underwear and maybe your clothes.

My advice is often to speak to an adult if it is happening regularly – perhaps it is the size and shape of the products that are not working for you, perhaps you are not changing it every 4 hours, perhaps a different product type is right for you.
I also advise wearing old underwear that you don't mind leaking on as you get used to having periods.

'Will I bleed to death?'

Many girls worry about the amount of blood loss. I show them a menstrual cup and pour around 2-3 cups full into a bowl. 80 – 100ml is considered to be the average blood loss.

This is around the average blood loss in a period. It helps them understand that it isn't that much. I also share that the 'blood' is not just blood, like when you cut yourself. It is made up of mucus, tissue and water too.

If they have excessive blood loss - filling more than one pad or tampon per hour, then there is an issue that needs checking by a medical professional.

There is more in depth information about menstruation in chapter 3.
Skin, Sweat and hygiene - Facts

The skin and scalp begins to secrete oils during puberty. This can create oily hair and greasy skin. Most people wash their hair as it starts to look greasy.

As the body goes through puberty it begins to create sweat. It isn't actually the sweat that smells, however, when it dries it is eaten by bacteria and this is what creates that sweaty smell.

Hygiene is really important here because if we don't wash that smelly bacterium stays on us. If we don't wear fresh underwear or socks or clothing then the bacteria will make our clothes smell.

It is a good idea to promote daily showers and show your child how to wash their body effectively to remove the bacteria.

However, be sure to teach them how to carefully wash their vulva. There is no need for douching and particularly scented products.
There is a delicate ph. balance in the vulva and vagina and they are essentially self-cleaning. A gentle wash on the vulva – the outer genitalia, is adequate.

It is likely that school will do lessons on hygiene as your child reaches the end of primary school. This seems to be the time that puberty is kicking in for all pupils and PE can become a smelly time!

Mood Swings - Facts

One of the effects of hormonal fluctuations is mood swings. Young people can feel dreadfully upset and unable to find a reason why one minute and then fine again the next or lashing out at their family in anger and then wanting to be cuddled on the sofa again like nothing has happened.

It can be really confusing for all around – young person included - when these fluctuations occur.

We often hear of the moody teenager but during puberty it really cannot be helped.

Some of the mood swings are linked to other bodily changes that are happening. They can be triggered by thoughts around being different from their peers and not knowing where they stand in the world anymore.

People treat them as a child but they feel more adult than before. They can feel very alone – not fitting in with their friends anymore.

For the child going through puberty there can be intense feelings of attraction or love and it can feel all-consuming and like no one understands. Puberty can be a really tough time for all children.

Common concerns

Children that I have worked with have found it really difficult to communicate to others around them what is happening at this time.

Whereas an adult may be able to verbalise what they need or what they are angry or upset about, the child going through puberty may just not know why it is happening.

They often find themselves grounded or in trouble for an outburst and feel a real sense of injustice. I'm not suggesting they should be let off when they react inappropriately but finding a way to communicate that they are having a hard time is key.

I have experimented with little cards that children can carry around that have some of the things they might need to share on it.

For example,
'Watch out I'm having a mood swing'

or

'I'm angry'

or

'Please leave me alone for a bit'

can be shown to a parent when a child cannot communicate their rage or feel intense desire to be alone.

Some children have written things like 'I need a hug' to indicate their desire not to talk about what is going on but just to receive some comfort. I've found that 3 - 4 cards are optimum.

There are a few you might like to use in the resource section at the back of this book. Their use must be clearly communicated to those they will be shown to in advance so that the trust between child and adult is kept.

It is by no means a perfect solution but it is one that helps the adults around understand what is going on for the child.

When I was a teen my mum and I would have almighty rows. Once we had one on New Year's Day. I fondly remember my dad saying, 'Well at least we have that one over and done with early in the year!' I would have really appreciated that space when I was in those moods. I would have also appreciated the space for a hug when I came back to a level emotional grounding.

It is important to remember that it isn't just the child being a grumpy teen. In-fact they may have no handle on what's going on for them at that time.

Attraction – Facts

We don't often consider attraction when we think of puberty.

The hormones racing around the body DO have a huge part to play in the way your girl might start acting around and thinking about others.

The hormones send signals to the body to start practising at 'being in love'. This is where the teen crushes on boy bands and 'that boy in class' come from.

There is a chemical reason for the 'intensity' felt by your daughter; it isn't just all flights of fancy.

As your girl grows she may find herself unable to get someone off of her mind. She may imagine what it is like for this person to hold her hand, to speak to them or to kiss them.

Sometimes this attraction is so intense that it almost physically hurts her. She may feel like her heart is breaking if the person she is interested in shows that they are not interested in her.

Common Concerns

It can be worrying to watch your girl in the throes of 'fancying' someone.

She is likely to be of an age where everyone else is just experimenting too and if she doesn't have her own boundaries and secure sense of self she may find herself being too intense or making decisions she regrets.

Some girls find themselves trying to kiss everyone; some find themselves always 'going out' with someone new and as they mature some girls find themselves entering into physical relationships with others earlier than perhaps we as adults might prefer.

I have created a separate chapter on relationships and intimacy. Although the chapter may be a hard read I ask you to cover it as your girl reaches 12/13 years of age.

There will be advice you can follow and things you can come back to as needed.

Coming back to the early days of puberty, at the age of around 10 or 11, your daughter might start fancying people.

She may even hold hands or have a kiss with someone.

It is useful before she reaches this age to have developed a strong sense of self and to know that she can speak up if she doesn't like something.

This can be as simple as talking about food, activities, films to watch and the like. Perhaps she comes home and moans about friendships and decisions made by others that affect her such as the way a team project is going at school.

If you invite and encourage her to give honest opinions on things and to stand up for these she can learn to give her informed consent throughout her life.

You can also support her in speaking up for herself and seeking support when things happen that she doesn't like.

As an example
– someone in the class walks by and pings her bra strap.

It makes her feel embarrassed and hurts.

She could just let it go or she could stand up for herself and tell that person exactly what she didn't like and that they shouldn't do it again.

She needs this assertiveness modeled and perhaps practised with you and other trusted family members.

You can set up activities where she needs to give her consent and speak up for herself.

Why not organise a day out that includes elements that you know she won't enjoy.

Encourage her to give her truthful opinion.

Speak to her when you know she is just saying 'yes' to keep the peace. Encourage her to find her voice and speak in a no-nonsense, firm and clear way.

When she feels the pain of 'heartache' be empathetic towards her.

Remember that for her this pain is real.

It is her first step into 'love'.

Support her with the love and care she needs rather than dismissing her feelings.

Chapter 3
Managing Menstruation

We absorb or collect the blood that is released using menstrual products. There are many different types of products available. Schools often get free packs to give to girls which may include a branded tampon and pad.

Most girls get no option regarding the products that they use. They are given the pads or tampons that family members use and may only ever get to experiment when they are in charge of their own money.

It can be really beneficial to have a look at a range of menstrual products with your daughter before she starts her period or when she starts her bleeds.

If you can, share a range of sizes and styles of products together.

You can talk about how they are used, experiment with some red food colouring, put on additional knickers and practice putting on pads and let her consider what she feels will be best for her.

You might want to get examples of:

Disposable	Reusable
Tampon without applicator	Menstrual cup
Tampon with cardboard applicator	Pad with popper connecting wings
Tampon with plastic extendable applicator	Period pants
Pad without wings	Menstrual sponge
Panty liner	
Pad with wings	

A list of organisations you can approach for samples that you can share with your daughter are in the resource page at the back of the book. This could save you from buying packages of each. Or chat to your friends to get one of their products and gather examples from a range of brands and types.

It is certainly worth speaking together about the positioning of products in underwear or internally and how your daughter may need a few goes to get it right.

When placed correctly cups and tampons shouldn't be felt. It can take some practice to get to this point.

I remember being on holiday in Center Parcs and wearing a tampon. I was in secondary school – I'm not sure how old. There is a huge pool with rapids and the like there. It makes up most of the holiday when you are younger. I went down those rapids feeling that tampon with every bump!

I just hadn't worked out how to get it in right and I could feel it all of the time. It also hurt to take them out – as they weren't in right in the first place.

Added to that was that it caused me so much discomfort. The additional worry of leaking as I knew it wasn't in right. But I wanted to swim. I wanted my holiday.

The same goes with pads – the length and shape can be important in terms of preventing leaks.

Who hasn't made the mistake of wearing a panty liner or little pad on a heavier day or one of the cheaper massive pads that doesn't really have the stickability required and it moving all over the place?

Having open and honest conversations about what is happening to your girl as she manages her period can help you both provide for her in a suitable way.

Feeling out of sorts during her period

Energy levels can fluctuate throughout the menstrual cycle. I like to liken it to the seasons we experience in the northern hemisphere.

Menstruation can be likened to winter – indoor, cosy, and less sociable.

Pre-ovulation – like spring –things are beginning to blossom and grow, energy is rising slowly.

Ovulation – as summer. We are feeling awesome, it is party time, we can stay out longer, be more sociable.

Pre-menstruation – like autumn – we are dropping the things we don't need, like autumn leaves, our body is beginning to slow down as …winter is coming!

Being mindful of these energy levels and social feelings and their fluctuations can allow you and your daughter to work with your bodies and not against them.

For example, it's someone's birthday party and you have just started your bleed. There is a long and energetic day ahead.

I'm sure you recognise that inner groan that would rise at this time when all you might want to do is stay home and chill in front of the TV.

But, if you know this is happening you might choose to turn up later, go for an hour and go home.

Anything that you can do to support your body and its needs is going to make for a better cycle in general. And if you can show this to your daughter, she too will be able to practice this cyclical self-care.

In my work with women I have seen this sense of self care, energy conserving and doing what the body really needs really reduce PMT and period aches and pains. It's like the body is moaning for you to stop for a bit and rest and if you do it, she stops grumbling!

For more information about the menstrual cycle as seasons and living a cyclical life see the resource section at the back of the book.

Chapter 4
Being prepared for periods

Although we won't know the exact day and time that your girl will start her periods there are some pointers that can help you to be prepared.

Around 2 years before her first period:

Breast buds appear
Pubic and underarm hair appears

Closer to the first period:

Discharge may be seen in the knickers
Mood swings
Body shape changes

As these signs appear it may be useful to create a 'be prepared' pack with your daughter.

This could be a funky pencil case or an understated wash bag that she can carry around in her school bag in preparation for her first period and the periods to come after that as her body establishes its cycle.

You may include:

Wipes
Pads
Spare knickers
Little disposal bag
Something to mark the occasion such as a little bracelet
Something nice to celebrate with – perhaps a piece of chocolate
A diary to mark her first bleed and perhaps her thoughts
A little note from mum
Some tissues

Remind your daughter that her first period is likely to be brown in colour. This is normal.

Over the next 6 months to a year her body will be getting to grips with its own cycle so there may not be regular patterns at first. It can take time for her body to establish its rhythms. Remember to re-stock the pack after each bleed so that she can continue being prepared.

Charting

To help with establishing a pattern and predicting menstruation you could teach your daughter how to chart her periods.

Perhaps this is something you might like to do together.

There is a range of ways that this can be done – there are many period apps out now. See the resources section for apps available when this book was published.

It is worth looking at these first as some of them focus more on fertility.

I have also included links in the resource section to diaries and period based charting journals and some downloads for menstrual charts. You can always use a regular diary or calendar.

The basis of all of these is noting down the first day of each period to establish how long a person's cycle is.

You can also note down the following and look for patterns:

When the period stops so you can establish the length of the bleed

Energy Levels throughout the cycle, such as when are you most energised and least energetic?

Emotions through the cycle including are there teary days, angry days, super happy days?

How social you feel, when do you definitely want to hang out with mates, feel studious or want to stay in bed all day?

Cervical Mucus, charting when is it watery, creamy or crumbly.

This will help you and your girl build a picture of what it is to be 'you' or 'her' through your menstrual cycle and help you notice any changes as they occur.

As she notices her more 'duvet days' or 'going out, out days' she can plan her life around her cycle. It will stop that going to a birthday party when your period is due blues.

Chapter 5
Tips on supporting your daughter

Raising the subject of puberty or periods can be nerve wracking.

We can wonder what to say or how to say it, how it will be taken, whether we will give the right advice at the right times and more.

Here are some tips to support you and gently remind you that just having a trusted adult speak to them about puberty and periods is so much more than many children receive.
So go you!

Only give facts

Sometimes, when we are in conversation and a question is asked it can throw us. It may be that we don't know the full answer or we think we know the answer but we haven't checked the facts.

It could be that we find the subject matter pretty tricky and could be that we just don't feel ready to give that answer yet.

Try to keep to the rule that 'If I don't know it as fact – I won't share it'.

Too many children are given part truths and completely wrong information by adults that think they are supporting them because they are giving an answer.

You can employ some really easy phrases to buy you the time to research or practice your answer.

Phrases such as:

'I'm not sure, let me find out and I'll get back to you.'

Or

'I need some time to think about that one. I'll get back to you.'

Both of these are truthful, they don't fob off your child and they give opportunity for more conversations.

It's important that you do go back to them with the right answers. If you don't go back at all you let the child down. They lose faith in you as part of their support network and may seek the wrong information from other sources.

Pull out the phrase, remove yourself and get Googling. Check many sites so that you know you are getting truthful info or go to the library and check a book.

Speak to them before the event happens

Sometimes we wonder
'When is the right time?'

In my opinion, the right time is before it happens.

As your daughter shows signs of starting puberty begin the chats. Tell her about hair growth and breast budding. Invite her to ask for help if she needs it. A little later speak to her about the next stage of breast growth and touch on periods.

Build a 'be prepared' pack together and chat about menstrual products as she goes towards that second year of puberty. Have a look at some on Pinterest and Etsy for some first period kits or menarche packs and enjoy the time together exploring this new phase for you both.

If you are reading this book and your daughter is already going through puberty still schedule some time for a mother-daughter date.

Work out where she is now.

Make sure you give her the support she needs.

Find out how she likes to receive this information

Ensure that you don't push it down her throat.

Some girls are really interested and lap up the information without squirming or looking embarrassed.

Some girls find it a bit uncomfortable to speak about these subjects and the content can worry them.

My advice is schedule in some time to do something together – go for a walk, do a jigsaw puzzle or bake together. – make time that will allow you both to be together in an informal environment.

Ensure distractions like ipads and phones are not in the vicinity. They are so easy to pick up and check out of the conversation with.

Tell her that you would like to tell her a little about what to expect as she begins to grow up this year.

Ask her what she already knows about growing up and let her know that when you are talking about this stuff you can use words you might not normally use together – like 'boobs' instead of breasts, etc.

As you start this conversation, gauge her reaction. Has she tensed up, is she looking shy or is she leaning in interested for more information straight away?

Ask her if she wants to speak about it now.

Ask her how she wants to learn about it – does she want to talk, look at books, draw pictures?

Try and accommodate her needs and help her feel comfortable.

Let her know that sometimes this kind of stuff can feel awkward to talk about and it is OK to feel embarrassed and have a laugh about it together.

But don't let her check out completely.

Explain that it is important to learn the real facts from someone who cares about her rather than things her friends might be saying that might not actually be true.

Create an atmosphere of trust and respect

Having someone to speak to about her worries, changing body, periods etc. is huge. It can really help your daughter as she goes through difficult times to have a role model, and a trusted one at that, to search for help from.

Share with her that you are always here to answer any question she might have.

Explain that she can come to you at any time with anything, even if she feels like it's embarrassing or uncomfortable to talk about.

Tell her that she can take her time and you will help whatever the subject is.

Make sure that when she asks for help that you give her the time and space and treat her with respect.

If you mock her questions she won't come to you with things that really need your help. If you don't make the time for her, she won't come to you and she will look for help elsewhere.

It really is a two way process and as the adult you are the one leading here.

You can orchestrate the time together.

You can organise the 'be prepared' pack making session.

You can be the light for your girl in this often murky and confusing time.

Chapter 6
What to do when the first bleed comes

So, it happens.

Your little one starts her periods.

Wow – what a big thing this is.

This has never happened to her before.

This is now something that will continue to happen to her for many years.

As I said before, having a conversation with your daughter before her first period is best practice. Find out what she would like to happen on her first period.

Ask her if she would like to do something to mark this special day.

We are all so different in the way we want to have things marked.

Some of us relish being the centre of attention and some of us really don't.

You don't want to make the mistake of creating a memory of where she felt uncomfortable. You want to support her transition in a way that feels smooth and supportive to her.

This rite of passage is celebrated in so many ways across the world - but it is your daughter's input that will make it special to her.

Maybe all she wants is some time with you. Perhaps this is a special lunch or dinner. Perhaps some time cuddling on the sofa. Or perhaps she would like a period party with all the important ladies in her life and her friends celebrating her, all wearing red and eating red velvet cupcakes!

If you can speak to her beforehand, and give her some ideas if she hasn't got any of her own, you can have a plan for this special day, this rite of passage – her menarche.

Ideas are:

Go out for a special dinner
Be given a special red necklace
Afternoon tea
A mother and daughter day
A pamper day
Spending time at the beach
Enjoying time snuggled up on the sofa with a good film
Bringing her breakfast in bed
Having a party with friends

Some mums like to prepare a special present for their daughter to mark her first period. If it calls to you perhaps you could gather together a few things to mark the occasion?
Perhaps a red box – or a box that reflects the girl it is for.

Fill it with things that will make this first bleed easier –

A pack of pads and perhaps some period pants or reusable pads

Some wipes
Spare knickers
A gel heat pack
A book on menstruation
A relaxation CD or playlist
A wash bag or pencil case to take these things
to school in

And some things to celebrate and remember
the day –

A red necklace
A red bead
A red badge
A letter from you
Some chocolate or treats
A journal to chart the cycle
A motivational postcard
A picture of her as a little girl and now

Remember also to remind her that you are
here.

If she wants to speak about the menstrual
products, or how she feels, or learn how to
chart her cycle in her diary she can always
come to you for help.

Chapter 7
Period Myths and Taboo Breakers

The amount of period based myths around is huge. Think about Chinese whispers – there is so much that happens as someone approaches and begins their bleeds that once children start talking about it it all gets warped and twisted and ends up as a fraction of the truth. Taboo too is rife around periods.

If you are able to have open conversations with your daughter you might get to hear some of these and actively challenge them.

But, if they don't come up from your daughter you can always put them into conversations using starters like

'Some people think that...'
or
'I heard some girls saying...x...on the bus...I wanted to tell you the truth here.'

Here is a list of commonly held misconceptions or myths to be aware of.

Myth/ Misconception	Facts
You can stop and start a period like having a wee.	No, the muscles in the vagina don't contract the way we can contract our urethra. We can't stop and start a period flow at will.
You can choose when to have a period.	No, the bleed comes at its natural point in the cycle as a result of hormonal changes.
Your period comes out of your wee hole.	No, the urethra is a tube that you can see when looking at the vulva and the entrance to the vagina. Period blood comes out of the vagina. They are different tubes.
People know when you are bleeding	Only if you tell them or you have a severe leak.

You can't swim on a period	You can and it is advised to wear tampons or menstrual cups if the flow is heavy.
All periods are supposed to be painful.	Periods really should not be painful. Anything that you might say was very painful could be a sign that you're not taking in the nutrients you need throughout the month, you're stressed, you've had some big life events happen recently or that there is something that needs investigating.
The egg comes out of you when you have a period.	No, the egg breaks down if it is not fertilised, so an egg is not present in the bleed. Perhaps particles of it are but these would be miniscule.

You can't get pregnant during a period.	A common myth that is upheld by many people. You can get pregnant during a period if the menstrual cycle phases are moving quickly.
You shouldn't have sex on a period.	There is no reason why not. It is up to personal preference.
Blood doesn't come out when you are in water.	Not true.
Tampons make you lose your virginity.	Virginity is defined as not having had sex. Tampons therefore won't make you lose your virginity. They may pull at or break an intact hymen but these are not always present.

Taboo around periods	
Periods smell	Period blood can have an irony smell. It isn't usually very strong. If menstrual products are not changed frequently enough and the blood interacts with the air, bacteria can form which create a smell (just like with sweat).
No one else should see a period	Why not? It won't cause any harm to anyone.
Periods kill flowers	In fact there are many reports of people who rinse out the menstrual cup or reusable pad and pour the water into their plants and see better growth in them.
Periods turn milk sour	No they don't.

Periods are unhygienic	Periods in themselves are a natural part of feminine life and so they are not unhygienic. Period blood however, is a personal secretion. As it has been inside someone's body it could potentially hold any germs or bacteria that the person holds.
No one should hear a wrapper of a menstrual product in a public bathroom	Why?
Anything to do with periods causing food to go off, animals to get sick, places to become dirty or soiled.	These are just not true. Just being in the same room as a menstruating woman will bring you and anything in the room no harm.

Depending on the background your family comes from there may be other myths around menstruation not mentioned here.

I think that in these cases you need to look at the myth or taboo.

Does it seem factual?

Is it something that you wish to uphold?

Do you think your daughter should believe the same?

If not, then you are in the prime place to make a difference here.

You can re-write the stories for your daughter.

Chapter 8
Relationships and Intimacy

This next chapter concerns relationships and intimacy. It is a brief introduction to the subject and mainly provides the key skills your daughter should own before she reaches the age of around 13.

I will be working on another book for supporting young teens with sexual relationships.

If you are reading this with an 8 year old daughter in mind consider where she is at right now compared to her being around 13 or 14. You have time to hone the life skills below so that she uses them as second nature.

Essential skills

For years before even speaking about physical relationships, I teach children to know themselves; their likes and dislikes and their goals.

I teach them to stand up for their opinions assertively and know how to get help when faced with pushy people.

I teach them to manage risks and to know that there are critical moments where you can walk away from things and you always have the right to do so.

And I foster the sense of self-esteem that comes from knowing your skills, knowing you are loved and cared about, knowing you have people to turn to and knowing that your body is perfect in its uniqueness.

The application of these skills can be translated to most life situations – crossing a road, choosing to steal sweets from the local shop, making a decision to lie to a family member and for intimate relationships.

Intimate relationships…remember the age of your girl now; if she's 8 or 9 just focus on honing the skills above.

If she is starting to fancy people read on.

We all have our stories around our first kiss, our first boyfriend and the first time we had sex.

For many of us, the first time we actually had intercourse with someone was far from the perfect ideal we had in mind. For many it was because we thought that it was the right thing to do. Perhaps we held onto the belief that this person would become our partner or would be with us forever.

Many of us would probably say we had sex first too young and perhaps we did other intimate sexual practices without really giving informed consent. Some of us chose to abstain, for whatever reason, and found taking that first step into a physical relationship hard to do and for some lucky women; we had the perfect experience with a loving partner.

What I am trying to say here is that it is hard to predict when and how a relationship will turn physical for your daughter and what that might entail. This is why the above skills need honing over the years before she reaches this level of maturity.

My main advice is talk about all kinds of relationships with her as she grows and talk about them more than once.

Speak about family relationships, loving partner relationships, relationships with friends and people that you see less often.

Talking about loving relationships can be the most difficult of talks but being open, honest and approachable will make those cringe worthy moments worth their weight in gold.

Talking about love and how it may be expressed in all of its forms provides a reference point for your daughter when she is thinking about her feelings towards others and the actions that may go with that.

No-one in my close family spoke to me about relationships, being loved, having sex or standing up for myself in a relationship. The only Sex-Ed I got was an ex-boyfriends dad saying to us, aged 16, that he didn't want any grandchildren just yet as we were about to embark on our college education. That was as far as it went. We had been engaged in consensual sex for a while before this talk.

If you are asked a question about physical relationships take a breath.

I find it is best to ask the child what they mean or why they have asked that question as our adult knowledge jumps to one conclusion when their question may have been a lot more innocent than we thought.

However, it might surprise you to hear that lots of 10 and 11 year olds have asked me about oral sex, same sex intimacy, abortion and sexually transmitted diseases.

Most of them know about or have watched porn and with the freedom of the internet images and videos are shared around group chats. Some 11 year old girls I have worked with have posted naked pictures of themselves on group chats.

This is not shared to bring about fear. It is shared to emphasise the need to speak to our girls and hone their skills before they encounter such chats and peer pressure.

So what do we say to the girls?

How do we approach relationships and sex?

The same as all the other puberty information in this book – be honest and be factual.
If you are asked about French kissing - say what kissing is and how we kiss our grandma in one way to show we love them or have missed them and how we might kiss our friends to say hello.

We may choose to kiss a romantic partner because we care about them and feel that we want to touch them and be close to them.

Sometimes we feel one way and the other person feels another way and that is ok. We do not always want the same things at the same time. This should be respected and is called giving consent.

Tell them factually that sometimes people choose to kiss and use their tongues.

It is likely to make your child look like they might be sick and ask why!

Again tell them factually that it feels nice to some people but it is up to the people involved whether they want to do that.

By talking about this they know that they can speak to you. They know they get truths from you and hopefully they will make decisions about who they choose to snog wisely.

When it comes to more intimate practices I always start with something like 'When two people have been in a loving relationship for some time'.

I feel that this adds to the sense of developing a relationship and not rushing into things.

I use the words 'sometimes' and 'may choose to' often because I want them to know that there is always a choice and nothing is set out as a 'must'.

It is important to share with your girl that she matters, that her thoughts and feelings matter, that her opinions matter. It is also important to teach her how to stand up for her opinions and thoughts and feelings and that she should not go along with anything that she doesn't want to and similarly that she doesn't put pressure on others.

If she asks about sex ask her what she knows already. Build on her knowledge factually. Tell her that some people who have been in a relationship for some time choose to have sex.

The law in the UK is that you have to be 16 or over to engage in sexual intercourse. It may be different where you are but sharing that age of consent is an important boundary for her to know.

Chapter 9
Continuing support for your daughter

Now you have a chapter on the facts of puberty, some additional information on periods and how to support your daughter as she begins her bleeds and you have some support for how to start conversations as well as buying yourself some time when you don't know the answers!!

Hopefully this is all you need to begin a culture of freedom of expression around puberty, growing up and periods.

Key things to remember are –

<u>She is probably as embarrassed as you</u> – This is a great space for growing in confidence together.

<u>Don't give up on her because she or you are struggling</u> -Keep at this in a way that suits you both

Don't let increased confidence run away with you

- If you feel good about starting conversations and answering questions that's great, but it can be easy to fall into the trap of answering with part truths because you 'think' they are right rather than 'knowing' they are right.

Always check the facts

- If you are unsure use a distancing technique and go and find out or perhaps check it out together!

Ensure that you keep the conversation flowing

-As she grows she will go through different stages of puberty. If you notice a new body change or mood change, make time to speak with her about what is happening.

Normalise what is going on

- Having these conversations as part of daily life will really support her sense of self as she begins to find out who she is in the world.

And finally….
Give yourself a pat on the back!

You are a trail blazer.
You are a 21st Century woman leading the next generation into a space where they love and understand their bodies…

Can you believe it?

What an honour!

I make a deep bow to you sister.

I thank you for all the work you are preparing to do and I invite you to share this book with others.

Let other women know it exists and that there is an active way to support girls through puberty and periods.

And please look out for my other titles for dads and daughters, mums and sons, the girls themselves and for teachers.

If you would like my support you can find me at my office at 58 South Molton Street, Mayfair, London.

In love, Melonie xxx

Connect with me on Facebook and Instagram @melonie_syrett and see what events and training I have going on for women and girls or join my mailing list at www.meloniesyrett.com

MELONIE SYRETT
Specialised Menstrual
Health Expertise

Resource Section
Useful websites and organisations

<u>Menstrual Product Suppliers:</u>
(This list is mainly reusable or organic options as disposable non-organic options are available in everyday shops. An internet search for reusable options and organic options will bring up many more than listed here.)

WUKA wear – reusable, machine washable period pants www.wuka.co.uk

Cheeky Wipes - reusable cloth pads and period pants www.cheekywipes.com

Precious Stars - reusable cloth pads, period pants, menstrual cups, wash bags and accessories www.preciousstars.co.uk

Mooncup - menstrual cup suppliers www.mooncup.co.uk

The Cup Effect - menstrual cup suppliers www.thecupeffect.org

Hey Girls - suppliers of organic pads, tampons and menstrual cups on a buy one give one model www.heygirls.co.uk

Moontimes.co.uk - eco menstrual products, books and gifts www.moontimes.co.uk

Places to approach to ask for samples of menstrual products:

Schools - from January 2020 schools in England will receive free menstrual products for all students. (Scotland already has this in place) These are likely to be mostly disposable products. They may allow you to have one or two to trial.

Community donation points - many small community collections take place and products are distributed to those in need. It is worth speaking to the organisers to see if you could make a donation in return for a product you have yet to use.

You could also approach companies, family members and friends.

Charting Apps and Downloadable Templates:

(Please use and evaluate these before giving to your daughter as they do include fertility and ovulation tracking. It is suggested that both of you have this app so you can talk about the patterns being shown and the features it has.)

Clue - app
www.helloclue.com

Spot On - app
Information and downloads from the App Store

Eve Tracker - app
www.glowing.com/eve

Flo - app
www.flo.health

Red School - Menstrual Dreaming Chart PDF
www.redschool.net

Eco Femme - Menstrual Cycle Tracking Chart PDF

www.ecofemme.org

madeincraftadise - PDF download printable period tracker
www.etsy.com

LemOnlinedesign - Moon Mandala, Moon Cycle tracker
www.etsy.com

N.B. There are many wonderful variations of cycle charts across the internet.

Searching using keywords such as 'period diary', 'period', 'printable menstrual cycle chart' and more will bring up a range of options.

Books on Puberty and Periods for Children and Parents

If there is no link it is because they are freely available from most book suppliers

Cycle Savvy - Toni Weschler
www.cyclesavvy.com

Reaching for the Moon - Lucy H Pearce

Hair in Funny Places -Babette Cole

Ruby Luna's Curious Journey - Tessa Venuti
Sanderson
www.cyclicalwisdom.com

Making Pink Lemonade - Sarah O'Mahoney
It's Good Being A Girl

Menstrual Doodles - Dr Rebecca Martin
www.amazon.co.uk/Menstrual-Doodles-
Rebecca-Martin/dp/0244712859

Beautiful Girl - Dr Christiane Northrup
Hayhouse.com

The Autism Friendly Guide to Periods - Robyn
Steward
www.robynsteward.com/books

The Period Repair Manual - Lara Briden ND

Period. - Natalie Byrne

Book Reviews

Sex Ed Rescue - A large online bank of Sex Education book reviews including bodies, disability, diversity and inclusion plus articles and information for parents
www.sexedrescue.com

The Real Period Project - Book reviews
www.therealperiodproject.org

A Mighty Girl - Blog
www.amightygirl.com

Moontimes.co.uk - a large book review collection ranging from puberty to menarche, self-esteem and body image.
www.moontimes.co.uk

Information on cyclical living and menstrual cycle phases

Red School - Wild Power (a book for adults) and information on the inner seasons of the menstrual cycle
www.redschool.net

Lisa Lister - Code Red and Love Your Lady Landscape (for adults)
www.lisalister.com

Maisie Hill - Blog on the four seasons of your menstrual cycle and her book Period Power (for adults)
www.maisiehill.com
www.amazon.com

Mood Swing Card ideas
- print/copy and cut out.

	I'm angry
	I don't want to talk right now Please leave me alone for a moment
	I need a hug

Printed in Poland
by Amazon Fulfillment
Poland Sp. z o.o., Wrocław

58470664R00083